UNSTOPPABLE

Row New Jersey Athlete's Handbook

Second Edition

KCM PUBLISHING

A DIVISION OF KCM DIGITAL MEDIA, LLC

CREDITS

Row New Jersey is Located on Lake Hopatcong, NJ, we are a 501(c)(3) non-profit corporation devoted to developing the strength, character and confidence of middle school and high school students as well as masters rowers, through the discipline and teamwork of rowing.

Unstoppable by Row New Jersey
www.rownewjersey.org

ISBN 13: 978-1-939961-87-7
ISBN 10: 1-939961-87-4

Photographs provided by Row New Jersey website and Facebook pages
Cover Art and Book Design by KCM Publishing
Authors & Editors: Rob Welsh
Contributors: RowNJ Board Members Stephanie Flower, Fred Sporer, Donna Marki, Vickie McCrink, Ken Beckerman, Krista Ruehle, Nicole Bennett, Nancy Priscu, Annabelle Hermey

KCM Publishing
www.kcmpublishing.com
The KCM logo is a registered trademark of KCM Digital Media, LLC.

KCM Publishing
a division of KCM Digital Media, LLC

Praise for Row New Jersey

"This team was instrumental in not only the development of my daughter as an accomplished athlete, but also as a diligent student and committed team player - invaluable life skills!"

"My son joined RowNJ as a freshman in high school. I thought for sure when he saw how much work and time it would take he would quit. Instead, he loved it. He stayed all four years, became captain as a senior and went to Nationals twice. He is still friends with many of his RowNJ teammates and was recruited to row for the Ivy League school of his dreams. He still loves rowing and his dedication to his university team was solidified through the work and input of his RowNJ coaches."

"Row New Jersey changed my son's life by adding a social and competitive dimension that he had not experienced before. He made friends, had fun, and worked his tail off to make it to Nationals. RowNJ gave him confidence, helped him to blossom, and brought him out of his engineering-based shell. THANK YOU Row New Jersey for completing my son's high school experience and for helping to shape him into the man that he is today."

"My daughter starts college this September. Tomorrow is her last regatta with Row New Jersey. She is very upset about leaving. This has been a wonderful experience for her. It has really changed her life! It's not just the sport; it's the coaches, kids and the board members that make Row New Jersey a special team. Thank you all so much for all you do to make this club what it is!"

"I just wanted to thank you for the last three years. I have learned so much about not only about this sport, but about myself. I'm a completely different person from when I started and I'm so happy with who I have become. I owe all of that to this team. I could not be more grateful for the experiences I have had, both good and bad. It was an amazing three years and I won't forget any of it."

"This sport has transformed by daughter in one year. She is more focused, has better grades and has made great friends."

To you, the rower, in pursuit of a worthy cause.

Contents

Preface

This book was created specifically for you, the athlete, to use as you see fit. It was intended to be useful in reminding you about the basics of the sport and answer questions, even for the experienced rower.

Most importantly, this is a workbook for you to use throughout the year.

The back of the book may be the most important aspect. Setting goals is something you have already started doing and will continue for the rest of your life.

Write your goals down, review them with your coaches, make progress, and adjust.

Log your erg scores and make a plan to improve them. Write down what happens at the regattas. What position were you in? How did it feel? How were the weather conditions that day? What worked and what didn't? What do you want to follow up on after the regatta?

There is a notes section at the very back of the book entitled Free Thinking. Write down whatever you want there.

You can file this book on the shelf or keep it in your bag and see if you can use it to improve yourself, your friendships, and your life.

"It is not the critic who counts; not the man who points out how the strong man stumbles, or where the doer of deeds could have done them better. The credit belongs to the man who is actually in the arena, whose face is marred by dust and sweat and blood; who strives valiantly; who errs, who comes short again and again, because there is no effort without error and shortcoming; but who does actually strive to do the deeds; who knows great enthusiasms, the great devotions; who spends himself in a worthy cause; who at the best knows in the end the triumph of high achievement, and who at the worst, if he fails, at least fails while daring greatly, so that his place shall never be with those cold and timid souls who neither know victory nor defeat."

— ***Theodore Roosevelt***

UNSTOPPABLE

www.rownewjersey.org

1

Row New Jersey

Located on the eastern coast of Lake Hopatcong, New Jersey, Row New Jersey is a 501(c)(3) non-profit corporation devoted to developing the strength, character and confidence of middle and high school students (grades 6-12), as well as masters rowers, through the discipline and teamwork of rowing. Row New Jersey is open to athletes from all schools in Morris County and beyond while catering to all levels of ability from novice to Division I college candidates. RowNJ strives to be fun while challenging all participants to achieve their very best. RowNJ seeks to help its athletes mature and prepare for life after high school by teaching teamwork, time management, dedication, and a sense of community. Finally, while participating in an activity sought out by many college recruiters, Row New Jersey athletes will experience the unbelievable beauty and power of being out on the water.

Row New Jersey has achieved several accomplishments of note:

- Two finishes in the top 5 at the USRowing National Championships in 2013 and 2014;
- Three top 10-in-the-nation finishes since 2015;
- One top ten-in-the-nation finish at the Head of the Charles Regatta in 2014;
- Six USRowing Mid-Atlantic Championships since 2015;
- In 2016, Row New Jersey qualified more crews for Nationals than any other program in the Mid-Atlantic Region;

- In the spring of 2019 Row New Jersey place three crews in the top 20 in the nation.
- In the 2019-2020 scholastic year, RowNJ alumni will be simultaneously racing at Cornell, Dartmouth, Syracuse, Penn, Santa Clara, St. Joseph's, Temple, Bates, Wisconsin, Washington Univ. - St. Louis, George Washington, Virginia and Yale.

Originally, this program was under the name Mountain Lakes Rowing Club. In Fall of 2019, the team changed named to Row New Jersey. The new name aims to attract potential rowers from across New Jersey. Row New Jersey serves the counties of Morris, Somerset, Union, Essex, Passaic, Warren, Hunterdon, and beyond.

Our program features a fleet of seven fours, nine eights, and three doubles and a single. Eleven of those shells were attained just in the last five years.

2019 Head of the Charles Regatta Varsity 8+s

2

What Will You Get Out of Rowing?

"One of the fundamental challenges in rowing is that when any one member of a crew goes into a slump the entire crew goes with him. A baseball or basketball team may very well triumph even if its star player is off his game. But the demands of rowing are such that every man or woman in a racing shell depends on his or her crewmates to perform almost flawlessly with each and every pull of the oar. The movements of each rower are so intimately intertwined, so precisely synchronized with the movements of all the others, that any one rower's mistake or subpar performance can throw off the tempo of the stroke, the balance of the boat, and ultimately the success of the whole crew. More often than not, it comes down to a lack of concentration on one person's part."

– Daniel James Brown

2016 Long Island Frostbite

The demands of rowing are such that everyone in a racing shell depends on his or her crewmates to perform their very best to achieve success. The movements of each rower are so thoroughly interwoven, so precisely synchronized, that the success or failure of a crew can never be achieved by one participant, even if they are a star athlete. A particularly strong or successful rower simply cannot offset a weaker one.

Therefore, a crew is only as strong as its weakest boat member. And each athlete must elevate one another to greater heights to taste victory. Such a team-wide dependence on one another for pacing, balance, and speed results in greater team closeness and dedication rarely seen in other sports where a collection of individuals can often thrive on their own respective talents.

Although previously confined to society's elite, rowing has exploded in the past two decades in popularity and participation. There are currently well over 100,000 people rowing across the United States. The majority of these are high school racers.

In addition, Women's Rowing has become one of the largest NCAA sports. Today there are hundreds of American collegiate programs, some of which offer scholarships, admissions help, or both. College rowing teams outnumber hockey, baseball, and lacrosse among others, often by wide margins.

The USA's second largest contingent of Olympians consists of rowers, trailing only track and field in roster size. The American Women's teams are the three-reigning Olympic champions.

Rowing is an activity in which you may continue to participate for their entire life. Many rowers row, and compete, well into old age.

Rowers experience deep levels of teamwork, commitment, motivation, and friendships.

From a conditioning standpoint, rowers are in some of the best shape from simultaneously using so many muscle groups. The legs, core, and arms are fully engaged for races that can last a mile or longer, necessitating heart and lung strength as well.

Socially, you will meet people from other towns in New Jersey and even all over the world. As a RowNJ participant, you will meet and race against other rowers from as far away as California, Seattle, Florida, and Canada nearly every season.

The essence of rowing is teamwork – not just any type of teamwork but the most unselfish kind there is. While you may compete for a spot in the boat every week, wherever you are placed, you have to psychologically adjust and come together as a team to row.

2017 Youth Nationals Sarasota, Florida

3

Goals and Values/Qualities in Athletes

"Nobody ever took time out in a boat race. There's no place to stop and get a satisfying drink of water or a lungful of cool, invigorating air. You just keep your eyes glued on the red, perspiring neck of the fellow ahead of you and row until they tell you it's all over... Neighbor, it's no game for a softy."

– Royal Brougham, *Seattle Post*

Here's the thing about rowing, you can't hide anywhere when you're in that boat.

The only option is to dig deep and find the mental and physical strength to be part of a team and perform. You can try to row faster or slower, but you will just mess up the cadence and synchronization of the boat.

It has been said that luck is where preparation meets opportunity. In order to perform as a rower, you have to have *prepared*, *shown up*, and *practiced properly*.

It is in the proper preparation that you develop the qualities of persistence and resilience required to perform at a superior level. You can achieve success by endlessly taking more and more strokes, either on the water or on land on the ergometer. There must be a goal or a point to be addressed with every stroke. That goal may be technical refinement of your stroke, an increase in one's physiological base, or some combination of both. For one cannot row properly without the proper aerobic foundation to do so.

2017 Youth Nationals Sarasota, Florida

4

Parent Responsibility

Harmony, balance, and rhythm. They're the three things that stay with you your whole life. Without them civilization is out of whack. And that's why an oarsman, when he goes out in life, he can fight it, he can handle life. That's what he gets from rowing.

*– **George Yeoman Pocock***

Parent's Viewpoint

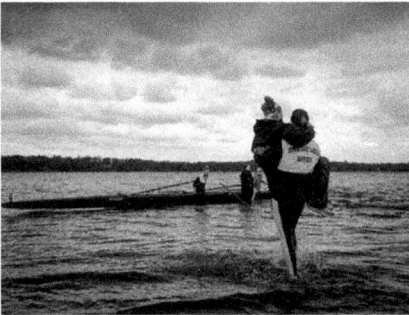

2016 Long Island Frostbite

Get ready for some significant changes in your routine. Rowing means long hours of waiting for brief periods of racing. Rowers and parents alike experience all sorts of weather conditions: wind, waves, sun, heat, cold, rain, hail, sleet, and sometimes snow! There is little time on weekends during the racing seasons to visit colleges or catch up on household chores. Your rower will be tired and sore after practice but will continue to go back for more. You will also probably notice a tremendous increase in your food bills, as rowing takes an enormous amount of energy and rowers need to refuel their bodies. But it also means you'll have a son or daughter who is physically fit and self-disciplined. They will have an unusual and attractive activity to list on their resumes. Your rower will increase his/her ability to work as a member of a team and will improve his/her capacity to strive for and achieve excellence.

Parent participation is critical to the success of the rowing program. Parents are encouraged to take an active role in supporting the RowNJ program. The rowing program cannot be successful without parental commitment to the following:

- Parents are expected to routinely check the website (www.rownewjersey.org) and read all of the emails from the coaches and the Board. All information pertaining to the team will be posted on the website. We also have a Facebook group (Row New Jersey Official Site) which shares lots of great photos, videos, and information about the team.

- Parents retain the ultimate responsibility for their child's transportation to and from practice. Carpools should be formed, when possible, from the varying high schools to the practice site. If upper classmen are driving lower classmen, with permission from the participating rower's parents, please be aware of the NJMVC's rules regarding the number of passengers permitted in your rower's car. The coaches are not responsible for monitoring any of the transportation to and from practice or regattas.

- There are many opportunities to participate. Parent volunteers are needed in virtually every activity of the rowing team. For example, parents are needed at all regattas to help with both the set-up and break down of the tents and food tables. Registration fees and dues do not cover all expenses required to operate the team. Due to the need to purchase/maintain costly rowing equipment and facilities, there are fundraising events scheduled throughout the year where volunteers are always needed.

- Parents are expected to remit all seasonal fees/forms by posted deadlines or their rower will not be able to participate.

Communication that parents should expect from the coaching staff:

- Practice schedule and locations
- Competition schedule, location, and race times
- Any injury that a student has incurred during practice or competitions
- Discussions about any issues that might or will require possible or intended disciplinary action including program exclusion

Communication and behaviors the coaching staff should expect from parents and/or rowers:

- Notification of any practice or competition scheduling conflicts (twenty-four hours in advance for missed practices, fourteen days in advance for missed competitions)
- Support for the program's activities and goals (student's on-time attendance at all practices and competitions, appropriate discipline regarding pre-competition rest and meals, emphasis on academic excellence and competency, assistance with any fundraising and volunteer opportunities as needed)

The appropriate concerns that should be discussed with a coach and the procedures for scheduling the discussion are:

- Discussions concerning a rower's skill development and improvement, academic eligibility or performance, behavior or conduct at school, practice or competitions
- Procedures for discussing concerns with a coach would be to schedule an appointment with the rower's immediate coach, via email, outside of practice hours or competitions

A note about fundraising:

Row New Jersey strives to keep fees as low as possible each season. Although RowNJ does receive some support through donors, it is simply not enough to ensure that the rowers have a rewarding experience, receive skilled training by competent coaches, and work with equipment that is safe and well maintained. RowNJ sets fees to cover stated costs only – we do not make a profit from team registration fees.

Unfortunately, the replacement of a shell costs is in excess of $35,000 or more, and all the other supporting rowing equipment (oars, ergs, cox boxes, launches, engines, truck, trailer, etc.) is also quite expensive, creating an ongoing financial responsibility. To cover these additional program costs, RowNJ relies heavily on the fundraising efforts of its rowers/parents. All athletes are required to participate in the fundraising activities that occur during the season(s) that he/she is competing. Fundraising dollars are used for these capital expenditures.

Advice for new parents:

Patience and support are two of the most important qualities a rowing parent can demonstrate. Rowing is a sport where its participants receive very little external recognition. Here are some ways that you can help your athlete and support the team:

- Try to attend as many regattas as possible. Most regattas are held at out of town venues. This makes it hard for other students to support the team and parents frequently make up the cheering gallery. Though some have more pageantry than others, all venues are attractive. Also, it's a fun way to meet other parents and to visit the region!

- Encourage your athlete to get adequate rest and eat a healthy nutritionally-balanced diet. Rowing is one of the most physically demanding sports. It demands high effort from all major muscle groups (arms, back, shoulders, and legs) and burns energy about twice as fast as running.

- Support your rower by becoming involved with RowNJ. Without your financial support and volunteer participation, the rowing program could not continue!

Coach's Advice

The sport of rowing requires significant time and commitment from parents. Thank them on occasion.

They rarely realize that when you sign up for rowing, they are getting signed up for the full rowing experience as

2016 Long Island Frostbite

well. There are things like a near-daily commute to Lake Hopatcong, cold-weather gear, warm-weather attire, medical paperwork to be completed and submitted, and feeding and nourishing an athlete with stamina requirements nearly unmatched by their peers. And all this happens while your brains and hormones are completing the extremely complicated, years-long process of transforming you from an adolescent to a full-fledged adult.

Cutting a check is the easy part. May you cut them a break too.

At times, they may be tempted to attempt to intervene on your behalf. While usually less than ideal, it's perfectly normal. Crew is relatively exotic in comparison to mainstream sports they played and understand. Now their child has developed a whole new language and often describes distances in meters. It's understandable they may have some questions if their child is repeatedly frustrated or disappointed with their progress in this time-consuming and expensive activity in which they know little.

Nevertheless, participants are encouraged to contact their coaches directly with questions or comments. After all, if a coach has made an honorable decision, he should have no problem explaining it either in person or in writing, even if it was a difficult or complicated judgment call. Just be prepared to handle the feedback in a mature fashion.

Parents, understand that there are not two sides to every story in which you are an independent, third party arbitrator. The coach is the expert and his or her point of view is not an opinion in which to weigh against your child's version of the fact.

Lastly, keep in mind that we, as coaches, do not pick the seats in the boats. The child does. With every practice attended or missed, every ergometer test completed, every stroke taken on the water, every positive or negative display of one's attitude, you are *persuading* a coach in the selection process.

Right or wrong, at the end of the day, you the athlete, have *convinced* the coach to make their decision one way or another. Both parents and children must remember that at the varsity level selection is often a zero-sum game. You may win a seat based on your own hard work and talent; just as frequently one may lose a seat to a peer's hard work and talent. Too often a dissatisfied participant or parent only sees half the equation.

5

Athlete Responsibility

"Good thoughts have much to do with good rowing. It isn't enough for the muscles of a crew to work in unison; their hearts and minds must be as one."

– George Yeoman Pocock

There are generally three rules to a successful rowing career at Row New Jersey:

1. **Show up on time.**
2. **Tell the truth.**
3. **Do not dishonor the team.**

Let's elaborate on the meaning of these rules briefly.

1. Showing up on time: Quite simply, this means you are where you are supposed to be when the coach expects you to be there. It is true you don't want to arrive late to Lake Hopatcong but this rule is about more than parking and getting oars down for practice in a timely fashion.

*Are you where you are supposed to be when
you are supposed to be there?*

That can be at the trailer before a race helping to put equipment away, not still in the bathroom when lineups are being assigned, ready and waiting when it's your turn to meet/launch/race at a regatta.

Everyone hits a traffic jam every now and then or has another factor outside of a participant's control.

Did you notify your coach about the issue in the manner and timeframe they requested?

2. Tell the truth: Nobody is perfect. Everyone makes mistakes. Accept responsibility for your shortcomings and you can still go far in crew and in life. Weaseling your way out of the mess rarely works.

You are often exposed, usually by other teammates and the situation will deteriorate quickly. If you overslept for practice, just say so. If there is a dance or concert you wish to attend, don't pretend you had a family emergency.

The rowing season is a marathon, not a sprint. You'll find your coaches surprisingly reasonable. If you are the kind of person who has established a pattern of solid effort and consistent performance for RowNJ, a mistake, poor decision, or other negative factor will not be fatal to your goals. But our team is too important, the sacrifices in time, seat, and money too deep, and stakes too high to entrust it to liars.

Win or lose, you cannot put a price on your character.

3. Bring honor to the team: One does not carve on rotten wood. Make decisions on and off the water that reflect well on Row New Jersey and you will always have a home here in our organization. Remember always and forever that you represent yourself, your family, and your community when you put on that uniform.

For many opposing teams, a regatta may be the only time they ever see, hear, or interact with anyone from Morris County, New Jersey, and our little piece of the planet overall. Fair or unfair, people will make judgments and generalizations based on those experiences.

If that does not persuade you, remember that you row for your coaches as well and the manner in which you do so reflects upon them directly.

We will not tolerate someone representing us who does not reflect our values. No one has ever grown wealthy coaching rowing. It is a labor of love for all your coaches from high school to the Olympic level.

I think you'll find that following these rules will serve you well not only in sports but in your lives and future careers as well.

2017 4th Annual Overpeck Regional Youth Regatta

Below is a list of responsibilities that ALL team members will follow:

1. Each athlete is expected to be at every practice on time, every day. If an athlete is consistently absent from practice, then they may be dismissed. If an athlete will be late, they must text their coach, but should NEVER DO SO WHILE DRIVING.

2. If an athlete is injured, they are expected to attend practice until such time as the coach says they may stay home.

3. Absence from practice because of a test, paper, or other academic responsibility is unacceptable. This may seem harsh, but everybody has an academic load to carry. Your

load is not any different or special. Managing your time is part of being a team member.

4. Athletes are expected to arrive at regattas on time. This does not mean arrival at the regatta, but instead means arrival at the trailer with your team. Please allow time for traffic and parking, especially if it is your first time competing at a new location.

5. You should never leave a team practice or regatta until a coach dismisses you.

6. Athletes are expected to treat the equipment with respect and handle the equipment carefully.

7. Athletes are expected to maintain the boathouse, training building, and property and pick up their personal items on a daily basis.

8. Athletes are expected to stay at a regatta and actively participate in de-rigging and loading until the trailer is fully loaded and ready to depart and the coach has dismissed the team or your boat.

9. Athletes are expected to advocate for themselves. If athletes have questions about workouts and boat lineups or have other concerns, they should speak with their coach.

10. Athletes will not use any social media or emails to violate the privacy of others, or to make disparaging statements about others, including coaches and other members of the team.

11. Consumption of alcohol or tobacco is explicitly prohibited.

12. If we feel an athlete is having a negative impact on this team we may suspend or dismiss that individual from the team.

6

Attendance

"Physiologists have calculated that rowing a two-thousand-meter race – the Olympic standard – takes the same physiological toll as playing two basketball games back to back. And it exacts that toll in about six minutes."

– Daniel James Brown

2016 Long Island Frostbite

Rowing is not like other sports. If someone doesn't show up for practice, it's sort of hard to run the boat. Certainly, you can have someone substitute for another but a four-person boat needs four people to practice effectively. An eight-person boat needs eight people.

The physical demands of the sport, as the quote above suggests, require an extraordinary level of endurance and resilience. These come from practice versus absenteeism.

Further, many athletes that came to the sport of rowing in high school are first time rowers and catching up. So that challenge that presents itself is one has to move quickly from learning basic skills to being able to compete at regional and national levels.

Participation in RowNJ is a commitment that, once decided upon, must be upheld. The coaches fully realize the time constraints that come with this commitment, but it is essential that team members be able to prioritize other activities to accommodate rowing.

Practices are mandatory. Acceptable reasons for missing practice are serious illness/injury, previously scheduled academic obligations (i.e. activities currently on the academic calendar which have been discussed with the coach), and religious observances. Medical appointments, heavy course load/homework, family outings, after school projects, last minute rehearsals, etc. should be scheduled AROUND your commitment, and every effort must be made to do so.

Part of what rowing teaches is how to effectively budget time and, through that, how to increase the ability to focus intently on the immediate task at hand. Additionally, it teaches that consistent effort while working towards long-term goals through delayed gratification will carry over into all aspects of your life and is a lesson you will take forward.

Another hallmark of rowing is the interdependence of teamwork. Individual absences could very well mean the difference between the rest of your boat going out on the water or staying on land. Everyone who joins rowing realizes they must respect the commitment the rest of the team has made in order for everyone to succeed.

In more realistic terms, if you miss a practice, it not only jeopardizes your seat in the boat, but the boat as a whole. And a boat affected is a team affected. Informally, what we're teaching is a work ethic. If you've got a serious injury, if you're sick, if you got a religious holiday, we're going to be ok with that.

Conflicts

Please notify the coaching staff as soon as you know of potential conflicts with school-related activities and rowing. Absences during holiday weekends and breaks that occur during the fall or spring season are not encouraged and may create a situation where a seat in a boat may be jeopardized. Few participants are completely unaware of the commitments of a varsity sport at their respective high schools. No one would dare tell their football coach they would be on vacation all week but not to worry, they will be back in time for Friday's kickoff. Likewise no one would tell their lacrosse coach they would be at the beach for spring break but look forward to getting back on the field upon their return.

It is essential that the coaching staff be given advance knowledge of these absences during the fall and spring seasons. Upon return, athletes will not necessarily resume their previous position on the team, and may have to earn their spot back.

So how sick is too sick to row? When in doubt, stick to the above-or-below-the-neck rule. For example, if your illness extends below the neck – e.g., gastrointestinal, stomach flu, food poisoning, diarrhea, etc., it's probably a good idea to avoid practice to recover. If the symptoms remain above the neck – e.g., runny nose, head colds, mild sore throats, eye and nose allergies, we'd like to see you push through it if possible.

Naturally, there are exceptions to every rule. Migraines can be utterly debilitating. Meanwhile, menstrual cramps are an inevitable part of any female athletic career. Use common sense to determine if attending practice in a given condition is right for you.

If you decide you are too sick to practice, return with a doctor's note. There are multiple reasons for this policy. First, coaches are not medical experts. Do not ask them for medical advice or opinions. A note from one's doctor directly informs a coach of a student's medical ailment so they may better understand how to proceed. Second, the note verifies for the rest of the team that no one is shirking their responsibilities. People legitimately fall sick. Doctors' notes ensure no one is avoiding practice in the bitter cold or on rainy, gray days only to magically recover in time for racing.

The note need not be from a doctor or specialist. It can be from the school nurse or trainer; however, it may not be from a parent.

Unfortunately, there will always be some parents who disagree with this policy, perhaps are even offended by it. Sometimes it is their decision to vacation or make other judgments that miss practice and will cover for their child as a result. Every year some parents will request a private audience with the coach to explain one situation or another. This is a mistake. Parents, if you do not like your child going behind your back, do not go behind theirs!

There is no hard number of absences that will dictate removal from one crew lineup or another. Selection is almost always a result of an ongoing analysis of a multitude of factors including attendance, punctuality, performance, and attitude. But if you must have a numerical target, strive for at least 90% attendance in the fall or spring if you expect to race regularly. Remember that the crew season is a marathon, not a sprint.

Over the year, there is ample opportunity to demonstrate what kind of athlete and person you are to your teammates and staff. The occasional academic, logistical, family, or social conflict is inevitable. You'll find that if you have built a consistent pattern of positive effort and performance over time, the occasional absence will not hurt your competitive prospects or place on the depth chart, even if that absence isn't for the noblest of reasons, such as oversleeping or a guilty pleasure social event. Again, refer to your athlete's responsibilities for telling the truth.

Coaches will be reasonable with an otherwise dedicated participant. Everyone needs to be cut a break once in a while. But if you are someone who has an issue every other week – travelling, then jetlagged and sick from all those airports, then you have to make up all the school work from all the travelling and subsequent illness, followed by an injury from inconsistent exercise, followed by an unrelated logistical issue and so on – expect your seat to be at risk.

Eventually a parent will try to frame the issue as unfair treatment when their child is replaced in the crew to making up a test after school while another got to go to the dance without penalty. But the whole truth is it was never that simple. The crew season is a marathon, not a sprint. Over time, you will all get a plenty of opportunities to demonstrate what kind of person you are and what kind of commitment you wish to make to our organization.

Coach Rob Welsh demonstrating proper use of the oar

7

Boathouse and Equipment

"George didn't just build boats; he also learned to row them, and to row them very well. He carefully studied the rowing style of the Thames watermen – a style characterized by short but powerful strokes with a quick catch and a quick release – and adapted it to the purpose of racing in a shell."

– Daniel James Brown

Interior view of Row New Jersey Boathouse at Lake Hopatcong, New Jersey

Part of what makes rowing an alluring, graceful sport is the equipment. Boats are differentiated by the number of rowers, the number of oars, and whether or not the boat has a coxswain.

When a rower has one oar that is a sweep oar.

When a rower has two oars, those are known as sculling oars.

The boats, known as shells, come in various sizes. A one-person boat is called a single scull.

A two-person boat can have two sweep oars (a pair) or four sculling oars (a double). A four-person shell with four sweep oars is a four; a four-person shell can be up to sixty feet long, but only weigh 150 pounds.

Oh, and by the way, these boats are very expensive.

They range in cost from **$35,000** and up. This is why, on occasion, you might hear coaches yelling or screaming at the top of their lungs, so you don't drop the boat.

The Boats – Sculls and Shells

All rowing boats can be called shells. Rowing boats with scullers in them (each person having two oars) are called sculls; e.g., single scull, double scull, quadruple scull. So all sculls are shells but not vice versa!

Originally made of wood (and many beautifully crafted wooden boats are made today), newer boats – especially those used in competition – are made of honeycombed carbon fiber. They are light and appear fragile but are crafted to be strong and stiff in the water.

The smallest boat – the single scull – is approximately twenty-seven feet long and as narrow as ten inches across. At fifty-eight feet, the eight is the longest boat on the water.

Interior view of Row New Jersey Boathouse at Lake Hopatcong, New Jersey

Oars

Oars move the boat through the water and act as balancers. Sweep oars are longer than sculler's oars and have wooden handles instead of rubber grips. The shaft of the oar is made of extremely lightweight carbon fiber instead of the heavier wood used years ago.

The popular "hatchet" blade – named because of its cleaver-like shape – is about 20% larger than previous blades. Its larger surface area has made it the almost-universal choice among world-level rowers.

The oars are attached to the boat with riggers, which provide a fulcrum for the levering action of rowing. Generally, sweep rowers sit in configurations that have the oars alternating from side to side along the boat. But sometimes, most typically in the 4- or 4+, the coach will rig the boat so that two consecutive rowers have their oars on the same side in order to equalize individual athlete's power.

2017 Youth Philadelphia Youth Regatta
(Picture of carrying a lot of oars)

8

Seasons and Distances

"'Nice? It's the ONLY thing,' said the Water Rat solemnly, as he leant forward for his stroke. 'Believe me, my young friend, there is NOTHING – absolutely nothing – half so much worth doing as simply messing about in boats. Simply messing,' he went on dreamily: 'messing – about – in – boats; messing –'"

– Kenneth Graham, *The Wind in the Willows*

Rowing is a year-round sport. The fall season typically has longer races than the spring. Winter in the Northeast is used for cross training, self-improvement, and goal setting. The following is a brief summary of what you should expect in each period of the year.

Fall

- Racing this season
- Practice will be on the water, if the weather permits
- Land practice will be substituted when water practice is not safe
- Athletes meet Monday through Saturday at the lake
- Race distance is often longer, typically 5000 meters, but sprint racing is also incorporated into the season

Winter

- No racing this season, only training at the gym
- This season the only focus is improving yourself, your erg times, and your strength
- Athletes meet Monday through Friday at a gym
- Activities range from strength training, boxing, swimming, cycling, yoga, and everyone's favorite: erging!

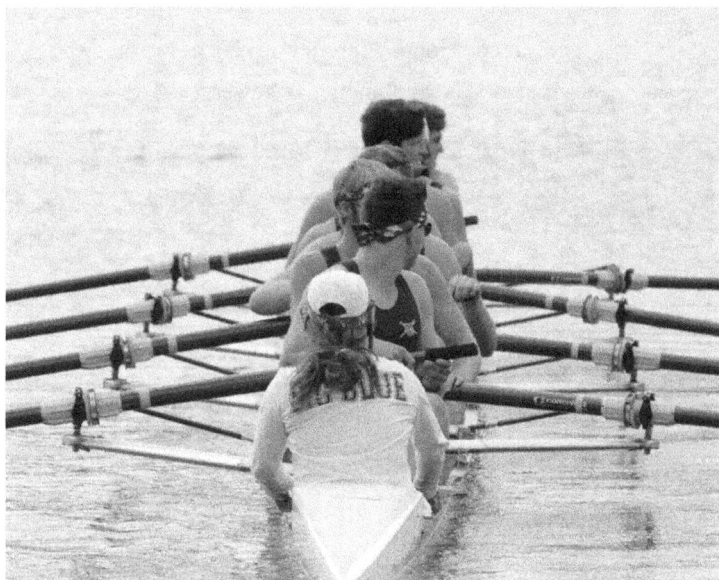

2017 4th Annual Overpeck Regional Youth Regatta

Spring

- Racing this season
- Practices are on water, rowing to improve technique
- When water is too rough, land practice workouts are substituted
- Athletes meet Monday through Saturday at the lake

- Races are head-to-head or occasionally time trials
- Race distance is 1500 or 2000 meters

Summer

- Racing this season
- Practice will be on water, if the weather permits
- Land practice will be substituted when water practice is not safe
- Athletes meet Monday through Friday at the lake
- Race distance is 2000 meters or lower

2017 4th Annual Overpeck Regional Youth Regatta

9

Crew Lingo

"Another paradox lies in the physics of the sport. The object of the endeavor is, of course, to make the boat move through the water as quickly as possible. But the faster the boat goes, the harder it is to row well...As the tempo accelerates, the penalty of a miscue – an oar touching the water a fraction of a second too early or too late, for instance – becomes ever more severe...In this sense, speed is both the rower's ultimate goal and also his greatest foe. Put another way, beautiful and effective rowing often means painful rowing."

– Daniel James Brown, *The Boys in the Boat*

Sculling – Each rower rows with two oars, one in each hand. In sculling the shell (boat) types are:

- Single (1X) – a shell for one sculler
- Double (2X) – a shell for two scullers
- Quad (4X) – a shell for four scullers

Sweep – Each rower rows with one oar, and each rower position in a shell rows from alternating sides. Most sweep shells may have coxswains. Shell types are:

- Pair (2+ or 2-) – a shell for two sweep rowers (the + or – notes whether a cox is in the boat or not).
- Four (4+ or 4-) – A shell for four sweep rowers (the +or – notes whether a cox is in the boat or not).
- Eight (8+) – A shell for eight sweep rowers with a cox.

Coxswain (pronounced coxen) or **cox** – The oarless crew member in a sweep boat who is responsible for steering and calling the commands. The cox either sits in the stern or the bow of the boat.

Bow – The front of the shell. The bow crosses the finish line first. When you sit in a shell, the bow is behind you.

Bow (seat) – The rower sitting in the front of the shell is called the bow and occupies the bow seat. In sculling shells, the bow steers the boat and gives commands.

Two (seat) – The rower sitting in front of the bow.

Three (seat) – The rower sitting in front of two seat.

Stroke (seat) – The person sitting in the last seat of the shell, closest to the stern. The stroke sets the pace. Everyone rowing behind the stroke follows his/her strokes.

Bow pair – The bow and two seat.

Stern pair – The stroke seat and the rower behind the stroke.

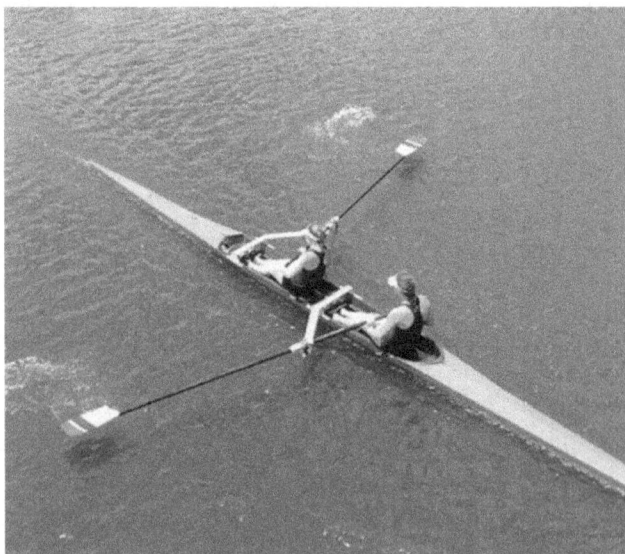

2017 Youth Nationals Sarasota, Florida - Sweep 2-

Stern – The back of the shell, which is in front of you when sitting in a shell.

Engine Room – Rowers in the middle of the shell. They are usually the biggest and strongest rowers in a boat.

Starboard – The side of the shell that is on the left-hand side while sitting in a shell.

Port – The side of the shell that is on the right-hand side while sitting in a shell.

Bow ball – A small white ball attached to the bow end of a rowing shell. It is used for safety and also to determine which boat crosses the finish line first.

Bow number – A card attached to your boat displaying the lane number assigned to the boat in a race.

Gunwales (pronounced gunnels) – The top rails on a rowing shell.

Oarlock – The square "lock" at the end of a shell's riggers where the oar physically attaches to the boat.

Rigger – Short for outrigger. It's the metal structure attached to the outside of the shell.

Skeg – A thin piece of fiber carbon under the shell that helps to stabilize the shell in the water.

Slings – Folding, temporary boat holders. Two slings are required to hold a boat. Slings are not to be used as seats!

Catch – The point of the stroke when the blades enter the water.

Drive – The propulsion portion of the stroke from the time the oar blade enters the water (at the catch) until it is removed from water (release).

Recovery – The non-work phase of the stroke when the rower returns the oar from the release to the catch.

Feather – To turn the oar so the blade is parallel to the water (the opposite of squaring).

Square – To turn the oar so the blade is perpendicular to the water (the opposite of feathering).

Crab (or "**catching a crab**") – A rowing error in which poor technique or slippage of oar handle in rower's hand leads to inability to remove or release the oar blade from the water, and the oar blade acts as a brake on the boat until it is removed from the water. This results in slowing the boat down and may require a near-stop to rectify. A severe crab can even eject a rower out of the shell or make the boat capsize. Occasionally, in a severe crab, the oar handle will knock the rower flat and end up behind him/her, in which case it is referred to as an 'over-the-head crab.' Avoid catching a crab at all costs!

Even pressure – The command for rowers to pull with even pressure on both oars.

Weigh Enough – The command to stop whatever the rower is doing – whether on or off the water.

Power 10 – The command to take ten strokes at hard pressure. Used for passing and gaining water in a race (sometimes power 5, 20 or 30!)

Heads - The command to raise a boat over heads. Or to look out for an approaching boat, as in "heads up"

Shooting the slide – When the oarsman's seat moves toward the bow faster than his/her shoulders. This is not good!

Ergometer (or "**erg**") – An indoor rowing machine.

2K = 2,000 meters. A 2K is a rower's fastest time rowing (or "erging") 2,000 meters on an erg.

PR or **personal record** – A rower's fastest erg score, usually refers to a 2K (i.e., "What's your 2K?" = "What's your PR?").

10

Boat Lineups and Position

"It is hard to make that boat go as fast as you want to. The enemy, of course, is resistance to water, as you have to displace the amount of water equal to the weight of men and equipment, but that very water is what supports you and that very enemy is your friend. So is life: the very problems you must overcome also support you and make you stronger in overcoming them."

– George Yeoman Pocock

Rowing shells (boats) are called by the number of rowers in the boat. Most novice rowers row in an eight person boat ("an eight").

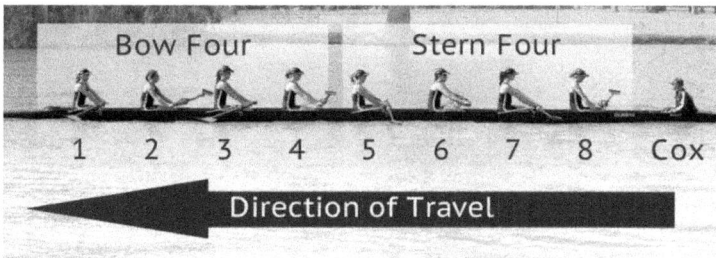

Illustration of "an eight" – side view

Starboard is a nautical term that mean the right side of a boat from the boat's point of view. Because rowers sit backwards in the boat, this can be confusing since the starboard side of the boat is on the

35

rower's left. Port is the term for the left side of the boat (on the rower's right).

Each rower uses one oar. Rowers whose oars extend from the right side of the boat are called starboard rowers or "starboards." Rowers whose oars extend from the left side of the boat are called port rowers or "ports."

Most rowers feel more comfortable on one side or another and usually settle into being a port or starboard rower. It is not uncommon for a coach to switch a rower from one side to the other – especially when the rower is a novice.

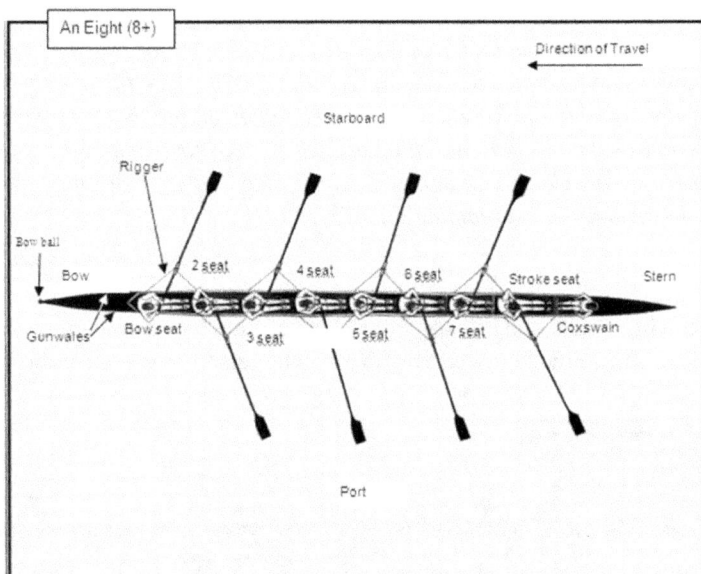

Illustration of "an eight" – top view

The general idea in rowing is for all eight rowers to be rowing in perfect unity, with no motions that interfere with the forward motion of the boat.

However, not all positions in the boat are the same. Each position has a slightly different role. Although, any rower should be able to row any position, the coaches will switch the rowers among seats to find out which rowers excel in which positions and which combination of rowers can move the boat fastest.

All the rowers need a combination of strengths: technique, rhythm, power, balance, and the ability to adapt to the motion of others. Each seat makes slightly different demands on the strengths of the individual:

- The **eight seat**, also referred to as **the stroke**, sits in the rear of the boat (or "stern") nearest the coxswain. Since everyone sits backwards, this is the rower that all the other rowers must follow in order to row together. The stroke must have strong technique (since the others are matching his or her motion) and a good sense of rhythm (since s/he is responsible for adjusting the stroke rate in response to instructions of the coxswain).

- **Seven seat** rows on the opposite side of the boat as stroke (i.e., if the stroke is a starboard, seven seat will be a port and vice versa) and, like stroke, needs strong technique plus the ability to mirror the motions of the stroke (but on the opposite side). All the rowers who row on the same side as the seven seat mirror his or her actions. Both the stroke and the seven seat together are called the stern pair.

- The **four middle rowers** (six, five, four, and three seat), while still demonstrating the combination of strengths, are generally the most powerful rowers, with six and five the stronger pair. You will sometimes hear the middle rowers referred to as the **"engine room."**

- The **bow pair** is made up of two seat and bow seat (who is for some reason not called one seat) and amongst the pair's other strengths, excel at "setting" or stabilizing the boat to ensure effective forward motion.

11

The Coxswain

"Ulbrickson knew what the real problem was...There were too many days when they rowed not as crews but as boatfuls of individuals."

– Daniel James Brown, *The Boys in the Boat*

Picture of coxswain

The coxswain or "cox" is the person in charge of the boat and the rowers, who sits in the stern (back) of the boat, facing the bow, and is the only person without an oar and the only person facing forward. Coxing is hard because there are so many varied responsibilities.

The coxswain is responsible for steering the boat and coordinating the power and rhythm of the rowers. In some capacities, the coxswain is responsible for implementing the training regimen prescribed by a team's coach during practice.

The role of a coxswain in a crew is to:

- Keep the boat and rowers safe at all times by properly steering the boat (according to the river or regatta rules and safety for the crew)

- Be in command of the boat at all times
- Coach the crew when the coach is not present
- Provide motivation and encouragement to the crew
- Provide feedback on the crew's performance both in and out of the races
- Make any necessary tactical decisions
- Organize and direct the crew at all times, including when putting the boat away, etc.
- Be responsible for the vessel; in the event of a collision, the coxswain is accountable under maritime law as 'Master of the vessel' (although the stroke may sometimes be the captain of the boat).

The coxswain is in charge of the shell. He or she is responsible for crew safety, which must be the prime concern. Along with steering, his or her role is to coach the crew. The cox acts as the coach's assistant, but in the absence of a coach, as is the case in a race, the cox becomes the coach.

Being in the boat, the cox has a feel for what the crew needs and a good view of technical errors. The cox needs to translate the coach's concerns into practical calls. The cox must be able to diagnose problems, such as balance and coach the crew into appropriate corrective action.

Picture of coxswain

At the start of an outing, the cox must be able to take the crew through a technical and physical warm-up so that the coach is presented with a crew which is able to start the training program and has recapped any points that the coach has been emphasizing in previous outings. It is essential that the coach and the cox work in good harmony and show respect to each other all the time. It's essential that the cox is briefed on what the coach wants to achieve in the outing from the point of view of building physical fitness, technical skill and team spirit.

A cox must be positive, a good motivator and very encouraging. Whilst errors must be spotted and corrected, it is also important to catch someone getting it right where they have been struggling.

Steering the vessel

Rowing boats are designed for speed, not maneuverability, so steering requires effort. Coxswains may steer with either the tiller (a cable connected to the rudder), commands for increased "pressure" or strength from rowers on one side of the boat, or both, depending on what is necessary in the situation. In the most extreme cases, the coxswain may go "full tiller," turning the rudder to its maximum angle, and may enlist the rowers to help the boat turn faster. This technique is usually reserved for only the sharpest turns, as the sharp angle of the rudder increases drag and upsets the balance of the boat.

For more conventional turns, the coxswain may move the tiller slightly to one side or the other over the course of a few strokes. To minimize disturbance of the boat's stability, the motion of the tiller must be smooth and not sudden. The coxswain may also initiate the turn during the drive phase of the stroke, when the propulsive force of the oar blades in the water helps stabilize the boat. For very small steering adjustments, the coxswain may move the tiller very subtly during the recovery phase of a single stroke. This technique is most effective at higher speeds and on straight courses, and must be used discreetly since motion of the tiller during the recovery can easily disturb the boat's balance.

Some coxswains advocate that the rudder should be applied only during the drive phase (and centered during the recovery phase), citing the fact that the boat is most stable when the oars are in the water and least stable when the oars are out of the water. The technique that often accompanies this view involves repeatedly moving the rudder back and forth over several strokes, making sure that the rudder is centered before every recovery. However, the rudder has much less steering power during the drive phase because of the very large forward propulsion force it must overcome. As a result, this technique often causes more boat drag due to longer rudder use, and the back-and-forth motion of the rudder tends to rock the boat.

The cox will also need to take into account the stream and the wind as well as the river. As a general rule, still waters do not run deep: rather the stream is strongest where the river is deepest. This explains why in the (Oxford and Cambridge) Boat Race coxes tend to steer in the center of the river. Competitive steering is best done by the cox steering their best course and leaving the other cox to make mistakes.

Cox-less boats

A boat without a cox is known as a coxless or "straight" boat. Besides the single and double, straight pairs and fours are the most common coxless boats at regattas in the US. Because of their speed and lack of maneuverability, eights without a cox are very rare and dangerous.

Weight

It is considered advantageous for the cox to be light – as there is less weight for the crew to move. However, weight is generally considered of minor importance compared to steering, coaching, and motivational ability. Nevertheless, most competitive coxswains weigh in at under 110 pounds for female coxes, and 120 pounds for male coxes.

US Standard

USRowing regulations require that a coxswain in an event for men's crews shall weigh at least 120 pounds and a coxswain in an event for women's crews shall weigh at least 110 pounds. It is permissible in certain regattas to have lighter coxswains, but crews are required to sandbag their shells to make up the difference.

US Junior

In the United States, junior women's crew coxswains are required to weigh 110 pounds. If not, they must carry sandbags to bring them up to that weight. Junior coxswains for men's crews must weigh a minimum of 120 pounds.

Cox box

Coxes in either coxed pairs, fours, quads, eights, or octuples can use a cox box, most models of which show the rate in strokes per minute of the person sitting in the stroke seat (the seat at the rear of the boat, from whom the rate of strokes per minute and timing is taken).

Additional features include:

- a stopwatch started automatically at the first full stroke
- stroke ratings over time
- GPS speed measurement
- Ratio of the power phase to recovery (speed of oars through the water versus returning out of the water for the next stroke)
- 500-meter split times
- Stroke count
- Metronome for stroke rates

However, the primary function of a cox box is to amplify the coxswain's voice, using a microphone connected to loudspeakers in the boat. This means that the cox needs only to speak for all rowers to hear his or her voice. For an eight man crew three or four speakers are set down the length of the boat; for a four-man crew, two speakers are used. Pairs may not have speakers if coxed from the stern but will have one if coxed from the bow (in front of the rowers). Historically, the cox would have carried (or strapped to their head) a conical, unpowered megaphone to amplify his or her voice.

General Guidelines for Coxed Boats

- The coxswain is in command of the boat at all times and should be given complete attention and respect.
- The primary job of the coxswain is to safely guide the boat by steering the boat and commanding the crew.
- Rowers of a crew should not talk while the boat is moving: it makes hearing commands difficult and distracts the coxswain from their primary job which is safely guiding the boat.
- Any rower who sees a hazard that they believe the coxswain does not see should notify the coxswain immediately.
- The coxswain is responsible for following the traffic pattern at all times.
- The coxswain is responsible for being aware of and avoiding other traffic – which may or may not be following the proper traffic pattern.
- If any rower hears thunder, he or she should notify the coach immediately. The sound of thunder is usually masked by the noise of the engine.

Coxswain's Calls

A good coxswain is just as important as the rowers and through good steering, calling a good race plan and motivating the crew can make the difference between winning and losing.

Check It Down

A call for all rowers to square their blades and drag them through the water in order to slow down or stop the boat. The call can also be made for certain rowers only, such as, "check it on port" or "stern pair check it down". "Check it down hard" usually means there is an emergency and the boat needs to be stopped immediately.

Hold Water

A call for the rowers to square their blades in the water while the boat is sitting still. This keeps the boat in a set place.

Let It Run

A call for all rowers to sit with blades off the water at the finish, allowing the shell to glide through the water.

Power 10

A call for the rowers to take "power" strokes, giving it everything they can for a certain number of strokes. This is used in races to make a move on another crew.

12

Weather Safety

"There is a thing that sometimes happens in rowing that is hard to achieve and hard to define. Many crews, even winning crews, never really find it. Others find it but can't sustain it. It's called 'swing.' It only happens when all eight oarsmen are rowing in such perfect unison that no single action by any one is out of synch with those of all the others. It's not just that the oars enter and leave the water at precisely the same instant. Sixteen arms must begin to pull, sixteen knees must begin to fold and unfold, eight bodies must begin to slide forward and backward, eight backs must bend and straighten all at once...poetry, that's what a good swing feels like."

*– **Daniel James Brown,** The Boys in the Boat*

Regattas

Regatta officials do not cancel regattas lightly; however, in extreme weather conditions, the officials may suspend racing on a given day until weather conditions improve or cancel a regatta altogether in they feel rowers' safety is at risk.

Weather conditions that may warrant the cancellation of a race or regatta:

- Sustained winds of 12+ knots or wind gusts of 15+ knots causing white caps in the water

- High probability of thunderstorms or evident thunder/lightning near race area
- Dense fog
- Extreme heat/cold conditions that can cause heat exhaustion or hypothermia

On the water, safety first is key. This applies to races and practices. If at any time a rower/coxswain feels at risk, the coxswain should notify the coach or race official. Both rowers and coxswain should remain alert of potential hazards and be aware of changing weather conditions.

2016 Long Island Frostbite

Perhaps you were wondering what a knot is and were afraid to ask. Here is how NASA explains it on their website:

Knots is how the speed of aircraft and boats are measured. Both miles per hour and knots are a speed, which is the number of units of distance that is covered for a certain amount of time.

1 knot = 1 nautical mile per hour = 6076 feet per hour

1 mph =1 mile per hour = 5280 feet per hour

For example, if a train is moving at 50 mph on a track, how would you represent this speed in knots (even though trains are not usually represented in knots)?

To do this problem easily, one must convert the speed in miles per hour that the train is moving to the speed in feet per hour. This is accomplished by multiplying by the number of feet in a mile.

That is,

(50 miles per hour)*(5280 feet/mile) = 264,000 feet/hour

Now, convert the feet per hour to knots by multiplying by the knots conversion factor (1 knot/ 6076 [feet/hour]).

(264000 [feet/hour])*(1knot/6076 [feet/hour]) = 43.4 knots

So knots are similar to miles per hour. Here is a simple chart:

Conversion table for knots to miles per hour

5	Knots	=	5.8	MPH
10	Knots	=	11.5	MPH
15	Knots	=	17.3	MPH
20	Knots	=	23.0	MPH
25	Knots	=	28.8	MPH
30	Knots	=	34.6	MPH
35	Knots	=	40.3	MPH
40	Knots	=	46.1	MPH
45	Knots	=	51.8	MPH
50	Knots	=	57.6	MPH

(seriously, you may really need this chart one day!)

2018 Nationals Pair

2018 Boat Launch

13

Erg Score

"The brutal afternoon workouts left him exhausted and sore but feeling cleansed, as if someone had scrubbed out his soul with a stiff wire brush."

— **Daniel James Brown,** *The Boys in the Boat*

Quite simply, an ergometer is a machine that measures **rowing power output**. It is also used to teach beginners the basic mechanics of the rowing stroke before heading out on the lake. For example, the proper motion of the arms, back, and legs as well as their order must be learned on land first in order to begin learning the process of successfully taking strokes on the water.

The machine itself consists of a seat in front of a handle and chain that spins a wheel. The wheel is linked with a small computer which records the speed of the wheel and displays the results on a screen in front of the participant. Feedback on the screen includes the pace of the rower for each individual stroke as well as the average pace of the entire assigned distance and strokes per minute of the athlete involved. Because of this instantaneous feedback of every single stroke, it is often easier to expand all one's energy over the assigned time or distance, resulting in the horror stories for parents about the extreme levels of fatigue on the ergometer relative to other athletic endeavors.

Each ergometer costs $900 and therefore must be treated and maintained as well as the fleet.

What are fast scores for 2k?

The standard testing distance in rowing is 2000 meters; however, it is far from the only distance a rower may attempt. Workouts can vary from multiple intervals of short, intense bursts of a few hundred meters or long, stamina-intensive intervals of 6000 meters or more. It is not uncommon for elite rowers to erg tens of thousands of meters every single week. At Row New Jersey, boys who wish to be considered for the varsity heavyweight boat should strive for a bare minimum of 6:45 or lower. On the lightweight side, boys should strive for 7:00 or lower while weighing in at 150 pounds or less. Females should strive for a time 7:45 or lower for the varsity category or 7:55 for 2000 meters in the lightweight category.

What are colleges looking for?

Because rowing has grown so much in the last ten years, erg standards have been raised considerably because of the growing competitiveness of potential recruitment. Erg standards for recruitment often vary from college to college; however, **NCAA-contending, Division I** women's programs will generally seek 2000-meter erg scores of 7:35 or faster. Male athletes should strive for times under 6:30, even at the lightweight level.

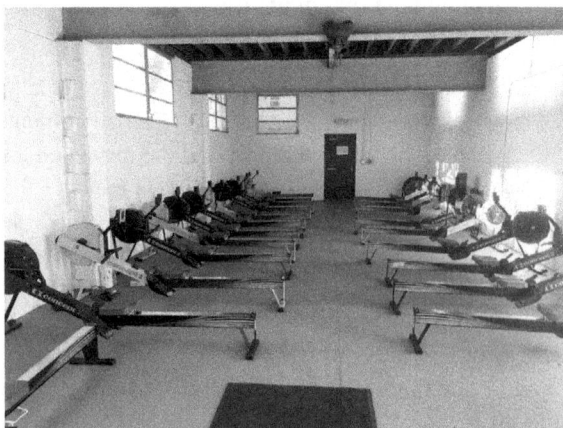

Interior view of Row New Jersey Boathouse at Lake Hopatcong, New Jersey

Ergometer testing

Ergometer tests are used by rowing coaches to evaluate rowers and is part of athlete selection for many senior and junior national rowing teams. During a test, rowers will row a set distance and try to clock the fastest time possible, or a set time and try to row the longest distance possible.

The most common distances for erg tests are 2000, 5000, 6000 or 10000 meters. The most common times for erg tests are 5 minutes, 20 minutes, 30 minutes, and 1 hour.

Results of these tests are an objective measure of an athlete's fitness; however, weight, technique, and team coordination also impact performance in a boat, so assembling a crew based purely on erg scores is not an optimal strategy. In fact, it is not unheard of for teams that are considerably faster on the ergometer to be beaten on the water.

Indoor rowing primarily works the cardiovascular systems with typical workouts consisting of steady pieces of 20-40 minutes, although the standard trial distance for record attempts is 2000 meters, which can take from five and a half minutes (best elite rowers) to nine minutes or more. Like other forms of cardio-focused exercise, interval training *is also commonly used in indoor rowing. While cardio-focused, rowing also stresses many muscle groups throughout the body anaerobically, thus rowing is often referred to as a* strength-endurance sport.

Unlike high impact exercises, which can damage knees and the connective tissues of the lower body, rowing's most common injury site is the lower back. Proper technique is a necessity for staying injury free, with a focus on both mechanics and breathing, as correct rhythm, exhaling on the drive and inhaling on the recovery, is a stabilizing force for the upper body. Non-rowers commonly overemphasize the muscles of the upper body, while correct technique uses the large muscle of the thighs to drive much of the stroke. Also, good technique requires that the angle of the upper body is never too far forward, nor too far back, both of which jeopardize the lower back and compression injuries on the knees and hip flexor muscles. In addition to the high levels of fitness attained, rowing is an intense calorie-burning exercise. Although rowers with less ability and training will burn fewer calories, the ergometer is an excellent tool for use in a weight-loss program.

The standard measurement of speed on an ergometer is generally known as the "split" or the amount of time in minutes and seconds required to travel 500 meters (1600 feet) at the current pace. A split of 2:00 represents a speed of two minutes per 500 meters, or about 4.17 meters/second (15.0 kilometers/hour). The split does not necessarily correspond to how many strokes the rower takes (the "rating") since strokes can vary in power.

Training Videos

Concept 2 has some basic training videos

http://www.concept2.com/indoor-rowers/training/technique-videos

14

Technique

"The greatest paradox of the sport has to do with the psychological makeup of the people who pull the oars...On the one hand, they must possess enormous self-confidence, strong egos, and titanic willpower. They must be almost immune to frustration...And yet, at the same time...no other sport demands and rewards the complete abandonment of the self the way that rowing does."

– Daniel James Brown, *The Boys in the Boat*

Proper technique is essential to successful rowing. Not only will superior strength and stamina be rendered by poor technique, but increase the chance of injury.

The entire body is utilized when rowing properly. But, in short, the rowing drive is approximately 60% legs, 30% back, and 10% arms. Flatwater racing bears very little resemblance to the notions of rowing such as the Roman slave galley ships of Hollywood or even lifeguard beach rowing.

The rowing stroke is a cyclic motion. The catch leads to the drive which leads to the release which leads to the recovery which leads back to the catch. Difficulty with one part of the stroke is often related to what is happening in a previous portion of the stroke.

For example, if you prepare the body poorly on the recovery, you may dive at the catch, which may cause you lift during the drive, sabotaging the entire horizontal nature of a correct rowing stroke in the process. If a rower is having trouble at the release, it is often due to a deficiency in the drive. Think of the hands as if they are on a very narrow conveyor belt. At the end of the conveyor belt, the hands fall gently down on the oar and the body begins to move away from the bow, pushing the hands away clear of the knees before they rise again.

Straying from the conveyor belt often results in one of the most common mistakes in rowing: burying the blade too deep. There can be many causes for this, but the result will be the same: a less effective drive. How does one know if they are digging the blade too deep? Look at the shaft of the oar during our row. If the water line is halfway up the shaft or more, you are digging the oar too deep.

One common solution to a compromised leg drive is to make sure you don't start the drive before you catch. Often the catch becomes part of the drive, putting too much pressure on the blade entry. Invariably the body will go up with the arms and oar will go deep. Catch, THEN drive. Keep the body still while catching with the forearms and remove the tension from the shoulders.

When oars go deep, we use smaller, less efficient muscles to do the work instead of hanging or suspending our body weight off the oar. Imagine a game of tug of war. You would plant your feet and lean your weight back against the rope – not up or down but horizontally back as your try to the other people across the line. Rowing incorporates the same concept. Remember, we are not actually moving the oar through the water much. We are moving the boat past the anchored blade. Once the blade is secured in the water, use it to pry the boat past. There are different weight classes in rowing because it can be an advantage to have more weight, but only if use that weight correctly.

2017 4th Annual Overpeck Regional Youth Regatta

2017 Mercer Lake

15

Boat Safety

"The speed of the racing shell is determined primarily by two factors: the power produced by the combined strokes of the oars, and the stroke rate, the number of strokes the crew takes each minute. So if two boats carrying the same weight have the exact same stroke rate, the one producing the more power per stroke will pull ahead. If those two boats have the exact same power per stork but one has a higher stroke rate, the one with higher rate will pull ahead. A boat with both a very high stroke rate and very powerful strokes will beat a boat that can't match it on both counts."

— ***Daniel James Brown,*** *The Boys in the Boat*

These boats are expensive but there is nothing more important than everyone's safety on the water. A submerged or partially submerged boat is a hazard to the immediate crew and other crews and boats.

Emergency Procedures
Never Leave the Boat!

- If you are close to shore and a strong swimmer, swim WITH THE BOAT to shore.
- Even if it is swamped or capsized, the boat will remain floating.

"Weigh Enough! Hold Water!"

- If you hear this, immediately square the blades and drag them against the water.

  - Do so no matter who gives the command – they might see something you do not, even if they are in another boat!

  - Act first! Don't look around – hold water first, before looking to see why.

Call for Help

In any emergency situation your first step should be to call for help.

- Yell for help, do not assume people can see you or recognize that you are in an emergency situation.
- Wave both hands in the air.
- Wave a shirt, or even an oar to signal distress.
- When possible, stay within hailing distance of the safety launch.

Person Overboard

The most common reason to fall out of a rowing shell is as a result of a serious crab. Keep in mind that the rower may be injured from the force of the oar. He or she may require someone to enter the water and provide immediate assistance.

- Immediately yell: "Weigh enough, hold water!"
- If a coaching launch is nearby, hail it immediately.
- An oar may be used as an emergency flotation device. If possible, use the rower's actual oar.

  - Remember that the oars provide stability to the shell and take care not to allow the shell to flip as you undo the oarlock.

  - Take care not to injure the person in the water as you send the oar towards them.

Collisions

- Is anyone in either boat injured?
- Is the boat damaged? If so, is it taking on water? If so, proceed immediately to shore or the nearest dock bringing the boat with you if possible.

If a person is injured, consider the following:

- Is there a coaching launch nearby? Someone should immediately try to flag down or hail for assistance.
- Does the person require immediate first aid?
- Is anyone in the boat qualified to administer aid?

If there is no launch nearby, and the injury requires attention, where is the closest help? This may depend on where you are on the river, and what time of day it is. Some of the possibilities for getting assistance include:

- Using a cell phone.
- If you are able to reach the shore easily, flagging down a passing vehicle may be the fastest way to get help. Take care to avoid being run over.

Shell Swamped

If the shell fills with water to the gunnels, the boat will still float but may break apart if the rowers remain in the shell. Take the following steps if help is not at hand or on the way:

1. Yell, "Weigh enough!"
2. Untie your shoes.
3. Rowers should buddy-up in pairs. The coxswain should buddy with the stern pair.
4. One at a time, the rowers should slip into the water, keeping hold of the boat for floatation.
5. Remove the oars or place them parallel to the hull. Loose oars will not only impede flipping the boat back over, but they can pose a hazard. Don't let the oars float away.

6. Move to the ends of the boat so as to avoid falling riggers and oars when your roll the boat over.

7. Roll the boat over.

8. Swim the boat to shore.

Once the boat is rolled, rowers may grasp hands across the boat. If the temperature is cold, lying across the boat, with as much of the body out of the water as much as possible is important as loss of body heat occurs twenty-five times faster in the water.

Shell Capsized

Capsizing is extremely likely in a small boat (single, double, or pair) and much less likely in a larger boat. Independent scullers should familiarize themselves with the procedure to right a boat and re-enter from the water. Larger boats (fours, eights) or if you are tired, cold, or unclear how to re-enter a boat, should be swum back to shore.

Once you are in sufficiently shallow water to stand, you may right the boat and get in. In any event, do not leave the boat! Even a swamped or upside-down boat will not sink.

A single or double, when righted, will generally have sufficient flotation to be rowed. Many such boats are designed so that much of the water will spill out immediately. Larger boats will need to be bailed out before being rowed. Remember that water is heavy and a boat full of water may break apart if you are not careful.

To Right a Capsized Boat:

1. Immediately make sure all rowers and coxswain are accounted for.

2. If you are in a team boat, buddy-up. Coxswain should buddy with the stern pair.

3. Grasp hands across the boat.

4. Swim the boat to shallow water or shore before attempting to right the shell.

5. Get control of the oars. Loose oars will not only impede flipping the boat back over, but they can be hazardous. Either put them parallel to the hull, or take them out. If the oars are removed, do not let them float away – you will not get home without them.

6. Fatigue and hypothermia can set in quickly in the water. If the temperature is cold, lying across the boat out of the water as much as possible is important as body heat loss occurs quickly in the water.

7. Re-entry from deep water is a complicated procedure that should only be tried if you are familiar with how to do so or are supervised by a coach.

We thought this was a cool image

16

First Aid for Rowers

"The sport offers so many opportunities for suffering and so few opportunities for glory that only the most tenaciously self-reliant and self-motivated are likely to succeed at it."

– Daniel James Brown, *The Boys in the Boat*

The biggest problem rowers face in the first year or so are blisters. Blisters are part of rowing and comparing blisters is a common rower activity. We have found the best thing is to keep them clean, leave them uncovered during the school day so they dry out, and then put Band-Aids on them while rowing. There are lots of new types of Band-Aids that can be found in any drug store to help.

While it may be frightening at first, blisters turn into callouses and are not a frequent issue once your child has been rowing for a while.

If a blister is raw and open, try to keep it dry and put antibiotic ointment on it to keep it from becoming infected, a great but painful treatment is called New Skin (can be found at any drug store), it burns while going on but creates a new layer of skin and it will feel better almost instantly.

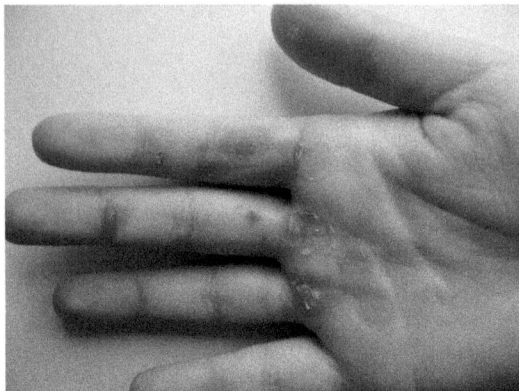

Random blistered hand.

Hyperthermia

Hyperthermia occurs when there is an increase in body temperature, usually when the air temperature is above 76 degrees and the victim is exposed to sun and heat in combination with a decrease in fluids. It may occur when:

- sweat cannot easily evaporate
- the body is being heated by the environment
- water-loss from sweat and respiration is not replaced and dehydration occurs

Two serious conditions may result:

Heat Exhaustion

A serious condition, heat exhaustion can occur when someone exercises in the heat and sweats a lot. Possible symptoms of heat exhaustion include:

- Sweating
- Nausea
- Dizziness
- Vomiting

- Muscle cramps
- Feeling faint
- Fatigue

Victim should lay down in a cool place. Remove as much of the person's clothing as possible. Cool victim with a cool water spray or damp, cool cloths to the neck, armpits and groin. Offer sports drink or similar liquid, or water if no sports drinks are available.

Heat Stroke

Heat stroke is life threatening! You must act quickly. Symptoms may include:

- Confusion, behavior changes
- Dizziness
- Feeling faint
- Unconsciousness
- Seizures
- Nausea
- Vomiting
- Muscle cramps
- Fatigue

Get medical assistance as soon as possible, call your emergency response number. Put the victim in cool water if possible. Check if the person needs CPR.

Hypothermia

Hypothermia, a serious condition which can cause death, occurs when a victim is subjected to cold temperatures, cold water, ice, or snow. Hypothermia can develop even when the temperature is above freezing.

There is potential for hypothermia if people are submerged in water with temperatures below 80 degrees. Water temperatures below 50 degrees are extremely dangerous. Hypothermia can even occur with air temperatures in the 60's, particularly if rowers are wet, exhausted, and exposed for long periods of time. Always obtain medical assistance as soon as possible when dealing with hypothermia.

Symptoms may include:

- Skin cool/cold to the touch
- Shivering (shivering will cease if body temp is VERY low)
- Drowsiness
- Confusion
- Apathy, lack of concern about situation
- Lethargy
- Stiff muscles
- Cold, blueish skin

Actions if cold and shivering:

1. Get out of the cold/water quickly (on top of a capsized boat for instance).
2. Keep as much of body out of water as possible.
3. Move to shelter quickly if possible.
4. Remove wet clothing; put dry clothes on person, if possible.
5. Phone emergency response number. Wrap person in clothing, towels, anything to keep the person warm (use other warm bodies if necessary) and cover head as well, but not face.
6. See if person needs CPR.

CALL FOR MEDICAL ASSISTANCE AND PROVIDE CPR IF NECESSARY.

DO NOT RE-WARM EXTREMITIES!

DO NOT PLACE HOT PACKS IN CONTACT WITH VICTIM'S SKIN.

17

Clothing

"Great crews may have men or women of exceptional talent or strength; they may have outstanding coxswains or stroke oars or bowmen; but they have no stars. The team effort – the perfectly synchronized flow of muscle, oars, boat, and water; the single whole, unified, and beautiful symphony that a crew in motion becomes – is all that matters. Not the individual, not the self."

– Daniel James Brown, *The Boys in the Boat*

The standard uniform for rowing is the men's and women's unisuit. There are styles for both warm and cold weather. Uniforms are required for all regattas. All athletes must have a unisuit (uni), cold weather top, and cold weather tights. Only RowNJ logo wear is allowed be worn in the boat during races.

2017 4th Annual Overpeck Regional Youth Regatta

18

College Recruiting/Rowing in College

"In an age when Americans enjoy dozens of cable sports channels, when professional athletes often command annual salaries in the tens of millions of dollars, and when the entire nation all but shuts down for a virtual national holiday on Super Bowl Sunday, it's hard to fully appreciate how important the rising prominence of the University of Washington's crew was to the people of Seattle in 1935."

*– **Daniel James Brown,** The Boys in the Boat*

For those interested or just plain curious about the subject, the following is a basic outline of the college admissions process from the aspiring rower's perspective. The process can be intimidating but can certainly be navigated with proper preparation.

Rowing is a large part of the collegiate athletic scene and rowing teams are present on the majority of campuses. They run the spectrum from the recreational rowing club to the super-competitive, multi-million-dollar armada, and everything in between. There are literally hundreds of college rowing programs, making it more popular than all but a handful of sports.

Many of these programs recruit from junior teams to fill their ranks. Some, like public universities from major athletic conferences (i.e.

major state schools), offer athletic scholarships. Others, like the Ivy League, offer help with admissions.

Before you read further, think long and hard about whether the college recruiting process is for you. Be warned, college teams, even small ones, practice six days per week from the first day of classes to weeks after the spring semester has ended. Many practice twice per day. Coaches will have little tolerance for your absences, poor performance, and various other excuses. They expect a level of commitment that far exceeds anything you have experienced at the junior level. There are a lot of new things to experience in college... some good, some not-so-good. But you will not have time for many of these activities if you are rowing.

If rowing is something you are unsure about, do not feign commitment and enthusiasm. Your uncertainty is perfectly understandable. Apply to college normally and if you later wish to give your all to crew, trust me, your college team will give you a good and fair look. There is always a seat available for someone willing to work hard.

If you know crew is your thing, you will want to do the following.

1. Keep the following in mind: College teams care about three things in the following order:

Height: Nothing you can really do about this. Choose your parents wisely. But fair or not, college coaches prefer kids with the most potential who they can "coach up." For open weight females, 5'7" and up is preferred. For heavyweight men, 6'2" and up is desired. Lightweights for both genders can be more varied based on individual coaching preferences. This does not mean that if you don't meet such standards you should give up on ever rowing for college. Plenty of rowers shorter than this are walking around with Olympic medals. But you better be prepared to compensate in the other categories.

Erg score: The 2000m erg test is the SAT score of rowing. No matter where you are, how good your team is, etc., the erg is the same everywhere. No matter your current technique or experience, most college coaches plan to convert you to their rowing style anyway.

But the erg is an objective measure not only of your power and fitness level but also your commitment to the sport. If you're willing to endure the practice, pain, and preparation that go into pulling a top 2k erg score, they feel more inclined to trust you to give that effort once you arrive on campus.

Grades: Many top college rowing teams are also academically selective. College admissions will take your rowing credentials into consideration to one degree or another depending on how hard that coach is fighting for you but they will not completely deviate from their normal academic standards. Rowing is not a revenue-generating sport. As such, coaches love promoting someone who is likely to succeed at the school anyway. Furthermore, for better or worse, rowing is generally centered around more affluent communities. Such competition is generally well-prepared academically anyway and you need to keep pace with students from top schools in other parts of the state and the nation.

2. Start early.

You generally want to come up with a preliminary list of colleges by the summer after your junior year. Don't put this off. Once you've completed it, visit the schools. Go to the athletic department's rowing webpage and fill out the prospective athlete questionnaire. NCAA regulations will often prohibit college coaches from contacting you until August before senior year; however, that doesn't mean they don't want you to contact them!!!

No college rowing team has the budget of Alabama football or Duke basketball. If you do not approach them, they do not have the means to find you themselves! This is especially the case since we are somewhat isolated from the Boston to D.C. corridor where so much rowing takes place. Contact them. Be proactive. Ask them questions. Demonstrate your interest. Don't have your parents do it. Don't have your coach do it. Colleges want to see you putting in the time and effort to showcase your enthusiasm. And don't just leave a message and hope for the best. Call back. Call again. Then send another email, just in case.

If any interest is returned, you will want to take official visits to the college in the fall of your senior year. Show up, spend a day or a weekend there, meet the coaches, watch a practice, etc. and don't forget to conduct yourself appropriately at all times. Many a promising recruit has blown their chance because they "enjoyed" themselves too much on such a visit. It doesn't matter that current students were also having a rowdy time. They are already admitted. You are not. Everything you do and don't do during your trip will be a topic of discussion after you leave and be absolutely certain your Facebook page and any other online presence you may have will stand up to scrutiny. They'll check. It's standard protocol for college recruiters. Just making it "private" will not suffice. The recruiters have too much on the line to risk something like this and there are ways around that stuff anyway.

If you believe you have found a good match, you should strongly consider applying early. There is nothing that coaches hate more than putting forth lots of time and effort and clout on behalf of someone only to have them choose another school. Applying early makes a strong statement of your commitment to them and their program. They are more likely to go to bat for you if they know you are fully committed to them. That being said, early admission policies have changed dramatically in the only the past two years and you should be very careful you fully understand exactly what the policy is and your chances might be for a specific school.

And yes, they will contact RowNJ coaches and ask about you. Don't worry about it. RowNJ coaches consider it part of their job to portray you in the best possible light to colleges; however, be aware they will not lie for anyone. That means, they won't tell a college coach you went 6:20 on your last 2k when you actually went 7:20. If you show up on campus as a different person than how you represented yourself and/or shortly quit rowing thereafter, it tarnishes our coaches reputation and the credibility of this program. What's more, it could damage the chances of future applicants from RowNJ who are genuinely interested in rowing for that team. Always conduct yourself with integrity and things will work out. There is nothing wrong with never picking up an oar in college. We have had students recruited to Princeton, Cornell, Georgetown, Penn, Cal, Wisconsin, Yale, USC, URI, and Temple and the two best kids RowNJ ever coached never rowed after their senior year of high school. It's a big world out there.

And finally, try to have some fun with the whole experience and not take the process too seriously. You never know where your rowing and college experiences will take you. There were no Harvard or Yale grads in the USA gold medal 8+ in Athens or bronze medalists in Beijing. There were, however, rowers from Temple, Oregon State, Ohio State, Northeastern, UT-Chatham, and Wisconsin. Great rowers come from unlikely places all the time. Don't fall in love with one program too early.

And finally, keep in mind that we are all one busted knee or broken shoulder away from an abrupt end to your athletic career. Pick a school that you think will make you happy and suit your career needs regardless of rowing. No matter how glorious, the athletic shelf-life is short. Someday you'll be turning pro in something else for a very, very long time. So enjoy these days. It may be hard to believe, but you'll miss them when they're gone. After all this info, if you still want to run the gauntlet, read on and good luck!

19

Drug Policy

"The 1936 crew, with Hume at the stroke, rowed with abandon, beautifully timed...They were a classic example of eight-oar rowing at its very best."

– George Yeoman Pocock

The NCAA Sport Science Institute released the following guidance in 2013 on the impacts of alcohol on athletic performance.

Consequences of Alcohol Use on Athletic Performance

- **Decreases aerobic performance.** Alcohol is a diuretic that can lead to dehydration. It also impairs temperature regulation and accelerates fatigue.

- **Impairs motor skills and decreases strength, power and sprint performance.** Alcohol slows reaction time and impairs precision, equilibrium, hand-eye coordination, accuracy, balance, judgment, information processing, focus, stamina, strength, power, and speed for up to seventy-two hours (three days).

- **Slows recovery**. Alcohol can interfere with recovery by delaying muscle repair.

- **Negatively affects body composition**. Drinking could lead to increased body fat accumulation due to ethanol storage as fat. Alcohol's stimulant effect can also result in increased caloric intake and, therefore, overall weight gain.

- **Increases the risk for nutrient deficiencies**. Not only does alcohol decrease vitamin and mineral absorption, but also certain nutrients are used to help clear alcohol out of your system, leaving less of those nutrients available for normal function.

- **Increases risk of illness and injury**. Regular alcohol consumption depresses immune function and contributes to delayed healing.

- **Disrupts sleep**. Alcohol can interfere with sleep patterns by reducing time spent in deep, restful sleep.

Even a few drinks can nullify your hard work by erasing the effects of your workouts, reducing your endurance, and compromising your mental fortitude.

The key question is, do you want to make the personal choice to be at peak performance for your team or not?

Alcohol use impairs muscle growth. Not only does working out under the influence increase your likelihood of injury, but it can also impede muscle growth. Long-term alcohol use diminishes protein synthesis, resulting in a decrease in muscle growth. Even short-term alcohol use can affect your muscles.

Getting enough rest is essential to building bigger and stronger muscles; however, because drinking alcohol negatively affects your sleep patterns, your body is robbed of a chemical called human growth hormone, or HGH, when you drink. HGH plays an integral role in building and repairing muscles, but alcohol can decrease the secretion of HGH by as much as 70%.

Additionally, when alcohol is consumed in amounts typical with binge drinkers, it can reduce serum testosterone levels, a biomarker that is measured by InsideTracker. Decreases in testosterone are associated with decreases in lean muscle mass and muscle recovery, which can impair performance.

Alcohol also depletes your energy. After alcohol is absorbed through your stomach and small intestine and moves into your cells, it can disrupt the water balance in your body. An imbalance of water in your muscle cells can hamper their ability to produce adenosine triphosphate (ATP), which provides the fuel that is necessary to help your muscles contract. A reduction in your body's ATP can result in a lack of energy and loss of endurance.

Of course, it's not just alcohol but perhaps you get the point. Smoking, vaping, dripping, dipping, tobacco, drug use; none of this is good for any athlete.

RowNJ Viewpoint

RowNJ has zero tolerance for drinking, illegal drug use, and smoking.

Any junior member found in possession of alcohol or illegal drugs or found to be intoxicated or under the influence of illegal drugs during a RowNJ activity by a coach, officer, or chaperone, will be sent home with his/her parents. Any club member found to be in violation of this rule will have their membership canceled for the calendar year and forfeit dues, regatta fees, or deposits.

The sport of rowing places extreme demands on a person's cardiovascular system. Smoking is not only unhealthy; it compromises the performance of the athlete and any boat in which they race. Any junior rower caught smoking by any coach, officer, or chaperone, may be removed from the team.

20

Tips for Surviving a Regatta

"To be of championship caliber, a crew must have total confidence in each other, able to drive with abandon, confident that no man will get the full weight of the pull."

– George Yeoman Pocock

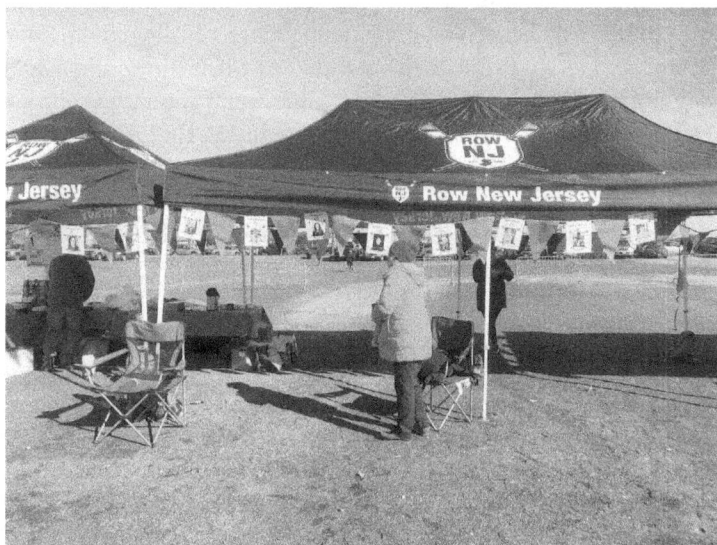

Typical tent setup for a Regatta

A collection of tips and strategies for having the best experience (as adapted from the Bainbridge Rowing Club's website):

- Go early and plan to stay all day.

- Parking is often limited at regatta sites so if you are scheduled to arrive at the beginning of a regatta, get there early.

- Be prepared to walk longer distances if you arrive later in the day. Some regattas do have police issuing parking tickets so pay attention to the signs. If you are transporting other rowers, you may have to stay all day as other rowers may be in races throughout the day.

- After the races are completed, the later scheduled rowers are expected to help put the boats back on the trailer, pack up the tents and equipment, and will not be dismissed until the coach says they are able to leave.

Dress for everything

No matter the time of year, a long regatta day can have all types of weather. The better you prepare, the more you'll enjoy the day. Mornings are almost always very cold and sometimes it's a long day in the rain. Take plenty of layers and warm socks. A change of clothes or shoes are often needed if it's raining. There is often mud even without rain. Bring a hat and a good pair of sunglasses – if the sun does come out you'll be looking at water and the reflection can be very strong. You can't bring too many clothes (at least the first time).

Bring anything you might need

At most regattas there are stores nearby, but a driving distance away and you do not want to lose your parking spot. Bring whatever personal items you might need, including your favorite snacks and drinks. Coffee will be provided at the beginning of the day, but the parents will be on their own for food. The kids will be fed at the trailer throughout the day with hot and nutritious food. Please make sure your kids are aware of their own food allergies and make it known to the people preparing the food, so they can be assured if there is any potential risk. Restrooms are often porta-potties so come prepared with toilet paper and hand-sanitizer if you prefer.

How to watch the races

We keep a white board in our tent to find race times. Your rower will walk with their boat down to the launch area about an hour before the race. If you go to that area to take photos, be careful to not get too near the boats and rowers as it can create confusion and distraction for the kids. During a Head Race, the next 45-60 minutes their boat will be off in the distance beyond what you can usually see. You will need binoculars to see the boats when they come down the course until the last 500 meters. Be sure to cheer them on as they do hear us from the boat! You will soon learn that taking pictures can be disappointing without a strong telephoto lens at some of the regattas where the kids are far away. Video cameras are also great to use as well, as the kids really like seeing their boat and can use the video as a learning tool as well.

What to do the rest of the day

Regattas are almost always very long days. The best way to pass the time is to volunteer and socialize with other parents. We need help with set-up and tear down, with food prep and service at the trailer where the kids are, and there is cleaning up as well. Sometimes parents are needed to run errands (pick up coffee, sandwiches, etc.). We will ask for volunteers before races via email if help is needed. Bring a chair, a blanket and even a book or computer to pass the time. At some locations there are great trails and paths for walking or running (Mercer Lake is excellent for this).

Keeping yourself nourished

The club provides food for rowers and coaches. In the past years, we would provide food for the parents, as we would be at the regatta all day long. Now the coach allows the kids to come closer to their race time, so the need to feed the families is not as important, especially since all regattas do have food tents (be forewarned – these aren't always healthy choices). Regattas are not usually in areas with stores in walking distance, so bring enough food and drink for a full if you are planning on staying the whole time. Bringing your own full water bottle is always a good idea.

Boat Area

The boat area can get very congested. It is meant for *coaches and rowers* who are rigging or de-rigging boats and getting ready for races. The coaches do not want parents to be at the trailer area, but if you need to speak with your child, please do not disturb them when the coach is speaking with them or if they are meeting with their boat in preparation for a race.

Clothing

Most large regattas sell T-shirts and other rowing gear. If you're interested, buy early as they run out of sizes by the afternoon. It's good to bring extra cash with you for vendors and parking as there won't be ATMs nearby.

Pack and load the car the night before. Help your rower prepare the first time but encourage them to be independent in their sport. Mark all their clothes, especially their unis, with their names. They should only carry one bag with their things – with lots of rowers it can get very chaotic and personal items often get lost. Many rowers bring homework to do during the time they're not racing.

Race Results

Race results will be posted immediately following a heat or race. The best sources to check boat times or placement, depending on the regatta are:

> www.herenow.com

> www.regattacentral.com

> www.usrowing.org

If it is a US rowing even, check the team website for the regatta host and there may be more information. For example: www.saratogarowing.com/head-of-the-fish

These sites are all very helpful in knowing how the boats really performed and how close the times were.

What to bring to a Regatta:

Rowers

> Uni and wrenches

> Team Hat and Team Jacket

> Team sweats and Team sweatshirt

> Cold weather training top and bottom

> Slip-on/off shoes for docks

> Waterproof shoes or boots

> Dry clothes for after race

> Socks – three or four pairs at least

> Homework assignments and books

> Phone / tablet and chargers

> Sunscreen

> Money – for T-shirts or food

Warm hat

Food for return trip

Blanket or sleeping bag

Parents

Sunscreen and sunglasses

Rain gear (including an umbrella)

Layers of clothing – temperatures can vary greatly from sunrise to sunset

Comfortable walking shoes

Binoculars

Camera

Chair

Phone / tablet and chargers

Headset

Blankets

Snacks, beverages, water bottle

Directions to the regatta

21

USRowing

"That is the formula for endurance and success: rowing with the heart and head as well as physical strength."

— George Yeoman Pocock

USRowing is a nonprofit membership organization and is the national governing body for the sport of rowing in the United States. The organization serves and promotes the sport on all levels of competition. USRowing is governed by a fourteen-member board of directors.

As a rower at Row New Jersey, rowers/coxswain must be a member of USRowing to participate in most regattas.

Membership options and benefits for Row NJ rowers:

Individual Membership – Basic

Basic membership enables athletes to complete a waiver and compete in USRowing registered (sanctioned) regattas. Benefits include:

- Online electronic registration and release form (waiver) required for an individual's insurance to be active
- Eligibility to compete in all registered regatta. Rowers must be Championship Members to participate in USRowing-hosted events

- USRowing *This Month* e-newsletter
- Sport liability coverage through the organization

Individual Membership – Championship

Championship membership provides national competition eligibility, discounts and educational resources. Benefits include:

- Eligibility to compete in USRowing hosted events; for RowNJ, this includes the Mid-Atlantic Regional and National regattas
- Free Subscription to *ROWING Magazine*
- 30%-70% discount on outdoor gear on www.experticity. com
- General liability insurance and excess medical coverage that follows you wherever you row even when your row independently
- Event access to conference, clinics, seminars – see US-Rowing event calendar for information
- Member discounts with participating partners (ex. United Airlines, Avis, Rubin Jewelers, etc.)

See www.usrowing.org/membership for more information.

22

Code of Conduct/Policies

"The true test of civilization is not the census, nor the size of the cities, nor the crops – no, but the kind of man the country turns out."

– Ralph Waldo Emerson

Below is the official code of conduct for Row New Jersey. Much of this is common sense, good manners, and respect. Rowing is a team-based water sport utilizing expensive equipment. This code of conduct was developed to ensure you have fun and stay safe.

ROW NEW JERSEY ATHLETE CODE OF CONDUCT

1. All athletes are expected to arrive at practice at least ten minutes early and be prepared to row or train on land. Arrival at the scheduled start of practice is LATE.

2. Athletes shall participate in all practices and regattas committed to. Athletes should review their schedules before committing to a practice schedule or a competition because missed practice will cause the athlete to be moved to a less competitive boat, and a late missed regatta will cause the athlete to be barred from competitive rowing for the season.

3. Athletes shall be attentive to coaches before practice to hear seating assignments and plans.

4. Athletes shall always have and display positive attitudes and a willingness to work with and encourage others. Abusive or derogatory language toward another athlete, coach, parent, another crew, or the power boater who just "waked" you will not be tolerated.

5. Rowers shall follow the instructions of any coach immediately. Disrespectful or abusive language or actions by athletes towards coaches, coxswains, parents, or members of the public at large will not be tolerated and constitute grounds for disciplinary action.

6. Talking in a boat is not just disruptive it is unsafe. The coxswain or bow seat in un-coxed boats is the only person who should be talking unless asked a direct question by a coach.

7. Athletes shall attend the entire practice or regatta unless they have advance permission of coach.

8. All athletes are representatives of RowNJ and the sport of rowing and should behave appropriately at all times. Congratulate competitors on a job well done after every race. "Good Race!" goes a long way towards creating good will. All comments about a race shall be held in check until the crew gets off the water and can sit down face-to-face with the coach to discuss the race.

9. Junior rowers must race in their team unisuit. Athletes are expected to show pride in their crew team by wearing team t-shirts, hats, jackets and hoodies.

10. All RowNJ athletes should take an active role in helping RowNJ crews prepare for races (help with shoes, oars, etc.) and RowNJ athletes should cheer on RowNJ crews whenever possible.

11. Socializing with other crews is an important part of a rower's career, but athletes must be available when needed by the team or coach. We attend regattas to compete.

12. Any violation of these rules or other actions deemed inappropriate at away races may result in exclusion from future races, or if severe enough, expulsion from the club.

13. Any junior member found in possession of alcohol or illegal drugs or found to be intoxicated or under the influence of illegal drugs during a RowNJ activity by a coach, officer, or chaperone, will be sent home with his/her parents. Any club member found to be in violation of these rules will have membership canceled for the calendar year, and forfeit dues, regatta fees, or deposits.

The sport of rowing places extreme demands on a person's cardiovascular system. Smoking is not only unhealthy, but it compromises the performance of the athlete and any boat in which they race. Any junior rower caught smoking by any coach, officer or chaperone, may be removed from the team.

ROW NEW JERSEY HAS ZERO TOLERANCE FOR DRINKING, ILLEGAL DRUG USE, AND SMOKING.

23

Board Function

"It was neck and neck now...Moch pounded on the ironwood as hard and as fast as he could...Hume took the beat higher until the boys hit forty-four. They had never rowed this high before – never even conceived it was possible."

– Daniel James Brown, *The Boys in the Boat*

Row New Jersey has a board composed of parents of current and past athletes. These parents give the limited time they have to keep the club operating. Know that there is a ton of effort going on to organize the sport annually.

Like many boards, the function is to establish vision, mission and values for the club.

- Determine the vision and mission to guide and set the pace for current operations and future development
- Determine the values to be promoted throughout the team
- Review and update goals
- Establish policies

Strategy and structure

- Review and evaluate present and future opportunities, threats, and risks in the external environment and current and future strengths, weaknesses and risks relating to the Club

- Determine strategic options, select those to be pursued, and decide the means to implement and support them
- Determine the business strategies and plans that underpin the Club's strategy
- Ensure that the company's organizational structure and capability are appropriate for implementing the chosen strategies
- Review and update bylaws
- Manage staff and facilities
- Work to assure continuity and growth of the club in keeping with its mission, vision, and goals
- Communicate with its members and guide the team & company

Positions of the Board

- President
- Vice President
- Treasurer / Bookkeeper
- Secretary
- Public Relations
- Parent Liaison
- Recruitment, outreach and succession planning
- Logistics
- Race day coordination
- Facilities
- Mission / Vision / Succession
- Photography
- Fundraising and event coordination
- Nutrition
- Publisher

24

Annual Registration

"The challenges they had faced together had taught them humility – the need to subsume their individual egos for the sake of the boat as a whole - and humility was the common gateway through which they were able now to come together and begin to do what they had not been able to do before."

– Daniel James Brown, *The Boys in the Boat*

Registration

To register for an upcoming season parents/athletes can go to www.rownewjersey.org and click on the "register now" button. You will be directed to the platform that RowNJ uses to help keep track of the team.

You will need to create an account. You can add yourself and any child that will be registering.

Once registered click on register to play/participate and you will be prompted to register for the upcoming season or event.

Sport Physicals

The state of New Jersey requires that each child that participates in a varsity sport have a physical on file with the school or club.

In order for your child to remain medically eligible to continue practice and competition throughout the entire year/season you will need to hand in a current physical form before the season starts.

The New Jersey pre-participation form can be downloaded at www.rownewjersey.org

Every child must have a current physical on file every year. Physicals are only good for 365 days and there is no grace period.

You will be reminded by email approximately three weeks before your physical expires.

Results from physicals can be emailed to the registrar or mailed P.O. Box 263, Mt. Arlington, New Jersey 07856.

25

Safe Sport

Policies

Athlete safety and well-being is Row New Jersey's primary goal. To facilitate that goal, we follow the direction of the U.S. Center for SafeSport, which is an independent nonprofit organization committed to ending all forms of abuse in sport. All athletes deserve to participate in sports free from bullying, hazing, sexual misconduct or any form of emotional or physical abuse. The Center provides policy guidance, education and support to teams like Row New Jersey on abuse awareness, prevention and reporting protocols to provide the best all-around positive experience for our athletes

In 2019, RowNJ acquired SafeSport policies, which is aims to abolish bullying, harassment, hazing, and emotional, sexual, and physical misconduct. This program is designed to assure athlete safety within the team. All reported SafeSport violations will be investigated and handled within the organization.

All coaches and board members of Row New Jersey are SafeSport certified. Row New Jersey's SafeSport policy can be found on the team website at www.RowNewJersey.org/safesport.

www.rownewjersey.org

Personal Logbook

Seasonal Goals

Year / Season (e.g., Fall 2017) _____

#	Goal	Progress	Achievement
1			
2			
3			
4			
5			
6			
7			
8			

Signatures:

Athlete: _____   **Coach:** _____

Year / Season (e.g., Winter 2017) _____

#	Goal	Progress	Achievement
1			
2			
3			
4			
5			
6			
7			
8			

Signatures:

Athlete: _____ **Coach:** _____

Year / Season (e.g., Spring 2018) _____

#	Goal	Progress	Achievement
1			
2			
3			
4			
5			
6			
7			
8			

Signatures:

Athlete: _____   **Coach:** _____

Erg Scores

Erg Workouts 1

Date	Rower	Distance	Time	Comments
9/2/2021	Indoor	2000 m	7:00 min	Felt sick, ear hurts from coach yelling

Erg Workouts 2

Date	Rower	Distance	Time	Comments

Erg Workouts 3

Date	Rower	Distance	Time	Comments

Erg Workouts 4

Date	Rower	Distance	Time	Comments

Erg Workouts 5

Date	Rower	Distance	Time	Comments

Erg Workouts 6

Date	Rower	Distance	Time	Comments

Regatta Performance

Fall

Date: **Regatta Name:**   **Location:**

Weather: **Conditions:**

Boat: **Position:**

What worked?

What didn't work or needs improvement?

What questions do I have for coach?

Date: **Regatta Name:**   **Location:**

Weather: **Conditions:**

Boat: **Position:**

What worked?

What didn't work or needs improvement?

What questions do I have for coach?

Fall

Date: **Regatta Name:**   **Location:**

Weather: **Conditions:**

Boat: **Position:**

What worked?

What didn't work or needs improvement?

What questions do I have for coach?

Date: **Regatta Name:**   **Location:**

Weather: **Conditions:**

Boat: **Position:**

What worked?

What didn't work or needs improvement?

What questions do I have for coach?

Spring

Date: **Regatta Name:** **Location:**

Weather: **Conditions:**

Boat: **Position:**

What worked?

What didn't work or needs improvement?

What questions do I have for coach?

Date: **Regatta Name:** **Location:**

Weather: **Conditions:**

Boat: **Position:**

What worked?

What didn't work or needs improvement?

What questions do I have for coach?

Spring

Date: **Regatta Name:**   **Location:**

Weather: **Conditions:**

Boat: **Position:**

What worked?

What didn't work or needs improvement?

What questions do I have for coach?

Date: **Regatta Name:**   **Location:**

Weather: **Conditions:**

Boat: **Position:**

What worked?

What didn't work or needs improvement?

What questions do I have for coach?

Summer

Date: **Regatta Name:**   **Location:**

Weather: **Conditions:**

Boat: **Position:**

What worked?

What didn't work or needs improvement?

What questions do I have for coach?

Date: **Regatta Name:**   **Location:**

Weather: **Conditions:**

Boat: **Position:**

What worked?

What didn't work or needs improvement?

What questions do I have for coach?

Free Thinking

Free Thinking

Free Thinking

Free Thinking

Free Thinking

Free Thinking

Free Thinking

Free Thinking

Free Thinking

Free Thinking

Free Thinking

Free Thinking

Free Thinking

Free Thinking

Free Thinking

Free Thinking

Free Thinking

Free Thinking

Free Thinking

Free Thinking

Free Thinking

Free Thinking

Free Thinking

Free Thinking

Free Thinking

Free Thinking

Free Thinking

Free Thinking

Free Thinking

Free Thinking

Free Thinking

KCM Publishing

a division of KCM Digital Media, LLC

www.ingramcontent.com/pod-product-compliance
Lightning Source LLC
LaVergne TN
LVHW051241080426
835513LV00016B/1703